Developing Strategies

Stefan Kühl is professor of sociology at the University of Bielefeld in Germany and works as a consultant for Metaplan, a consulting firm based in Princeton, Hamburg, Shanghai, Singapore, Versailles and Zurich. He studied sociology and history at the University of Bielefeld (Germany), Johns Hopkins University in Baltimore (USA), Université Paris-X-Nanterre (France) and the University of Oxford (UK).

Other Books by Stefan Kühl

Organizations: A Systems Approach
(Routledge 2013)
Ordinary Organizations: Why Normal Men Carried Out the Holocaust
(Polity Press 2016)
When the Monkeys Run the Zoo: The Pitfalls of Flat Hierarchies
(forthcoming)
Sisyphus in Management: The Futile Search for the Optimal Organizational Structure
(forthcoming)
The Rainmaker Effect: Contradictions of the Learning Organization
(forthcoming)

To contact us:
Metaplan
101 Wall Street
Princeton, NJ 08540
USA
Phone: +1 609-688-9171
stefankuehl@metaplan.com
www.metaplan.com

Stefan Kühl

Developing Strategies

A Very Brief Introduction

Organizational Dialogue Press
Princeton, Hamburg, Shanghai, Singapore, Versailles, Zurich

ISBN (Print) 978-0-9991479-2-4
ISBN (EPUB) 978-0-9991479-3-1

Copyright © 2017 by Stefan Kühl

All rights reserved. No part of this publication may be reproduced or transmitted in any form or by any means, without permission in writing from the author.

Translated by: Philip Schmitz
Cover Design: Guido Klütsch
Typesetting: Thomas Auer
Project Management: Tabea Koepp
www.organizationaldialoguepress.com

Contents

Foreword 7

1.
What Is a Strategy? Assembling the Means to an End 13

   1.1 Defining Strategies Using the Ends-Means Model 15
   1.2 Strategy as Part of Organizational Structure 19

2.
The Lure and Limitations of an
Instrumental-Rational Approach 38

   2.1 A Portrayal of Standard Procedure 38
   2.2 On the Popularity of an Instrumental-Rational Approach
       to the Strategy Discussion 40
   2.3 The Limitations of an Instrumental-Rational Approach 43

3.
Strategy Development beyond Understanding Organizations in Mechanistic Terms 61

3.1 The Emergence of the Approach 62

3.2 Searching for the Means to an End as well as
Searching for an End for Existing Means 66

3.3 Strategic Testing—Resolving the Divide between
Strategy Development and Strategy Implementation 68

3.4 The Process Architecture for the Development of Strategies:
The Resolution of the Classical Phase Model 71

4.
Concerning the Classification of Strategy Processes: Goals as a Characteristic of Structure, among Other Things 73

Bibliography 77

Foreword

Strategy is a concept that is taken for granted. It's on everyone's lips. There is hardly a business, administration, university, or hospital that appears willing to abstain from formulating a strategy. Executives are summoned to strategy retreats at regular intervals for the purpose of discussing the direction of their organizations. And in the meantime, curriculum modules on strategy development and implementation have become standard components of almost all MBA programs.

Although most strategy books look strikingly similar to the eyes of practitioners, we should not overlook the intense debate within the field of organizational science regarding the subject of strategic practices in organizations. According to the scholarly discourse on this topic, an understanding of organizations as machines continues to dominate classical strategic management, the strategic consulting firms whose activity supports it, and the tools they typically apply. It is claimed that classical notions of strategy view organizations only in terms of a single purpose that must serve as a measure for almost all organizational activity. Then, in order to achieve this purpose, strategy processes are used to search for appropriate means: "optimal communication channels," the "right programs," and "suitable personnel."

However, according to the criticism fielded by organizational science, things are unfortunately not that simple. Organizational reality looks quite different from the way it is portrayed in the idealized descriptions of strategy consultants. Organizations are frequently not clear about their own goals. The mission statements that are meant to provide orientation often only echo generalities that ultimately could be espoused in the same form by all of the organizations in the field. The employees in the various units and departments merely act as if they shared the organization's goal while pursuing their own specific interests. Life in organizations is said to be much wilder than the mechanistic understanding of organizations, which dominates self-help literature, would suggest.

The goal of this short book is to demonstrate what the development of strategies can be like when extended beyond a simplified, mechanistic understanding of organizations. Systems-theoretical organizational science informs us that goal orientation does indeed occur in organizations, but that it accounts for only one of many forms of structuring them. Rather than conceiving of an entire organization as an ends-means chain, we will show how the development and implementation of strategies can look when organizations are characterized by goal conflicts, by using goals as pure decoration, by shifting goals, and by end-means reversal.

In the first chapter, we define strategy as a process of finding appropriate means for a previously defined end. Drawing on systems theory, we integrate strategy development and strategy implementation in an overarching understanding of organizational structures. The second chapter presents three things: the form in which the long dominant school of strategy—the so-called Design School—subscribes to an instrumental-rational view of organizations; what makes this approach so popular; and why the instrumental-rational view of organizations comes up against its limits. In the third chapter, which also draws on innovations from critical strategy research, we then present how strategy development can look beyond an instrumental-rational understanding of organizations. The fourth chapter is a résumé of the book. It demonstrates why—in spite of all relativization that has by now become common in research—orientation toward a purpose must be viewed as an important form of structuring organizations, and how such purposive orientation in the framework of strategy processes fits into a systems-theoretical understanding of organizations.

This book was written primarily for practitioners in businesses, administrative bodies, hospitals, universities, schools, law enforcement, the military, political parties, and associations. The presentation of our methods is supported by many years of experience in strategy consulting for organizations. In specific passages, we repeatedly draw attention to the differences in the strategy development approach that we promote and methods that are frequently still common, and the form in which we link our approach to considerations based on recent organizational research.

Although the book was written for practitioners and is based on practical experience, we assert that the ideas we present align with the modern approaches of systems theory. Certainly, one must not disregard the fundamentally different utilization contexts and ways of thinking of organizational theory on the one hand, and organizational practice on the other. In principle, it will not be possible to eliminate the gap between organizational science and organizational practice (for management studies see Kieser/Leiner 2009).

Nevertheless, particularly in the third chapter, we endeavor to present a tried and tested method in such a way that its abridged definition of organizations does not immediately evoke condescending smiles from organizational scientists (e.g., see March 2015, 153f.). In the occasional passage, particularly in the first and second chapters (for example, when defining strategy from a systems-theoretical perspective or assigning a place to the strategy discussion within research on the limits of instrumental-rational organizations), we even attempt to go beyond the current status of research, thereby perhaps including ideas that may prove stimulating for organizational scientists.

In this book, we have refrained from describing individual strategy tools at length. The majority of strategy books repeatedly present more or less the same set of tools, from stakeholder analysis to SWOT analysis and the Blue Ocean strategy. In the meantime, there are a number of strategy books that do nothing more than provide a compact, although generally random, overview of tools. Readers who are interested in the ways familiar individual strategy tools can be integrated into our approach are referred to the "Metaplan Method Box," which is available online.

This concise book is part of a series that targets practitioners. Based on modern organizational theory, we present the essentials of a topic that is of central importance to managers. In addition to this volume, *Developing Strategies,* we will also publish books on the topics of *Designing Organizations*, *Influencing Organizational Culture*, *Developing Mission Statements*, *Managing Projects*, *Exploring Markets*, and *Lateral Leadership*. If a practitioner faces a specific problem within an organization, each of the books can be read independently. Yet the books also dovetail in such a way that reading them results in a coherent view of the way organizations function and the possibilities for influencing them. Since the books were produced in one casting, so to speak, attentive readers will repeatedly observe related trains of thought and similar formulations. This overlap is intentional and serves to emphasize the consistency of the underlying intellectual edifice and the cross connections between the different books.

We don't believe in simplifying texts for managers and consultants with clusters of bullet points, executive summaries, text-flow diagrams, or even with exercises. In most cases, such supportive features infantilize readers because they are based on the assumption that the readership is incapable of extracting the central ideas of the text without assistance. Consequently, in this book—as in all of our other books in the series—, beyond the sparing inclusion of graphics, we employ only a single element to facilitate reading the text. We have inserted small boxes to cite examples that concretize our thinking; we also use them to highlight links to organizational theory more extensively. Readers who are pressed for time or not interested in these aspects can skip the boxes without losing the train of thought.

The underlying principles for considerations on the development of theories were elaborated in *Organizations. A Systems Approach*. With respect to understanding strategy processes, we have specifically carried over our thoughts on goal conflicts, goals as window dressing, goal changes, end-means reversals, and searching for goals after the fact. The creation of detailed cross references is intended to show how productive the discussion of end-means models, which is being conducted so prominently in organizational research, can be for the discussion of strategy.

This book was developed in the context of a credential qualification program entitled "Leading and Consulting through Discourse," which is sponsored by the consulting firm of Metaplan. I would like to express my thanks to the program participants for repeatedly subjecting the approach presented here to critical examination, and for contributing the ideas and practical experience they gained in the field.

1.
What Is a Strategy?
Assembling the Means to an End

Hardly any other word in management circles is used as carelessly as the concept of strategy. We hear of strategies referred to as "courses of action for the future" (Schnelle 2006, 11ff.); as "a pattern in a stream of decisions" see Mintzberg (1978, 934); "a unique, new position that a company is striving to achieve" (Kolbusa 2012, 7); or as "some sort of consciously intended course of action, a guideline (or set of guidelines) to deal with a situation" (Mintzberg 2014, 3). Strategy is defined as "planned evolution" in a company (Kirsch 1997, 654), or as a plan "that integrates an organization's major goals, policies, and action sequences into a cohesive whole" (Quinn 2014, 9).

Since the word strategy suggests the future, people who are active in organizations often use this word to make something appear particularly critical for success. "Strategic purchasing management" carries more weight than simple "purchasing management," "strategic personnel management" lends the hiring and firing of an organization's employees special importance by relating it to the future, and using the term "strategy consulting" holds out the promise of higher fees for consultants than ordinary "organizational consulting." It seems that the word "strategic" can be placed before virtually any management concept in order to signal importance, although it remains unclear how the meaning of such statements would change if the adjective were simply omitted.

In view of the confusing usage of the word strategy, it is understandable that even in organizational science people attempt to approach the concept using the story of the blind men and the elephant. Repeatedly cited in discussions of strategy, this parable tells of a group of blind men who are trying to describe what an elephant is like by touching the animal. Since each one of them touches only one part of the elephant's body, their interpretations differ. Depending on which part of the animal's body they touch, they claim that an elephant is like a tree, a fan, a wall, a rope, a spear, or a snake. The well-known analogy also applies to the debate about strategy, where very different aspects emerge according to one's perspective (first mentioned in Mintzberg 1987). To one person, strategy appears as a plan with which the organization's challenges must be mastered; to another it is a pattern of behavior; and yet a third sees strategy primarily as the position of an organization within its environment. Someone else might use the term to denote the lens an organization uses to focus on the world (for the elephant parable, see Mintzberg et al. 2005, 2ff.).

Consequently, the great majority of monographs on strategy forgo a precise definition of the term. Even in a book bearing the title "What is Strategy" (Whittington 1993), the concept of strategy is not defined and therefore also not delineated from other concepts of organizational research. From the practitioner's perspective, the vagueness of the concept may not be a problem. Generating catchy phrases that can be interpreted almost at will by the members of an organization is part of everyday practice. Communications in organizations are so laden with terms that can be interpreted almost entirely at the user's discretion—"synergy effects," "proactive leadership," "win-win situations," "paradigm shifts"—that "strategic orientation" or "strategic management" attract no attention whatsoever. For an examination of strategy in greater depth, however, such random definition is problematic. If the concept of strategy remains undefined or poorly defined, it cannot be placed in relationship to other concepts that are used to describe organizational phenomena. For that reason, this book draws on a systems-theoretical perspective to suggest a precise definition of what practitioners mean when they speak and write about strategy.

1.1 Defining Strategies Using the Ends-Means Model

From a systems-theoretical perspective, strategy denotes the *process of searching to find the appropriate means to achieve a previously defined end*. From this perspective, *strategy formulation* (or strategy development) is the process of searching for appropriate means (see the early work of Schreyögg 1984, 246). *Strategy implementation* refers to the process of applying the means that have been identified as appropriate for achieving the previously defined end. *Strategy formation* refers to the means that form in the shadow, so to speak, of the official search process that is geared to an end.

It is only by using these precise definitions that one can link the strategy debate to the discussion of the relationship between ends and means in organizations, which is so relevant for organizational science (e.g., see the early contributions by Thompson/McEwen 1958; Perrow 1961; Luhmann 1964b; Gross 1969; Georgiu 1973). In organizational science, *ends*, or synonymously *goals*, refer to a precisely defined state that is to be achieved. *Means* are considered to be all of the possible ways this state can be realized. If ends are supposed to guide the search for means, which is to say, are to have a structuring effect in an organization, then they must be specified so precisely that one can ascertain whether the end has been accomplished or not. For that purpose, the following must be specified: the objective of the end (what is to be achieved?), the scope of the end (how much is to be achieved?), the time frame (when is the end to be achieved?), the personnel aspect (who is responsible for the end being achieved?), and the location (where is the end to be achieved?).

THEORY

In management books, the term "goals" is generally used in place of "ends." However, conclusive research in the field of organizational theory has established that distinguishing between the concepts of goals and ends does not make sense, and the two can be used synonymously.

When management literature discusses the character of goals, it is addressing the same questions as sociologists when they define the character of goal programs. Thus, examples of goal operationalization can also be read as typical examples of the definition of a goal program:

Objective of the goal: to increase market share
Scope of the goal: 5%
Timeframe: end of the current fiscal year
Personnel aspect: branch director, Southeast Asia
Location: regional market, Southeast Asia

Setting goals always represents a remarkable narrowing of an organization's horizon. It focuses the perspective of the organization on a small number of aspects that appear important, while screening out everything else. All goal setting focuses emphasis on one particular facet, but always at the cost of neglecting, if not even damaging, a multitude of other possible aspects. In that sense, goals—or ends, to use the other term—can be referred to as an organization's "blinders" (Luhmann 1973, 46). Just as horses have a very wide field of vision due to the lateral placement of their eyes, organizations, too, in principle, have the ability to expand their horizon almost at will. And just as blinders shield horses from distractions coming from the side or behind, goal setting prevents organizations from being sidetracked by a host of other options.

By setting goals, that is, by putting on blinders, organizations create a very simplified picture of their environment on their "goal screen" (Luhmann 1973, 192). If a company's goal is to become the market leader in computer hard drives, then it has no need to focus its attention on alternative markets such as displays or computer units. If the purpose of an army is to protect its own population from attacks by neighboring countries, then the commanders do not have to slate resources for alternative purposes, such as countering domestic insurgencies or preparing for military intervention in a foreign country.

This narrowing of the horizon through goal setting has another important function. It focuses energy on achieving the goal and mobilizes creative thinking on the best means of accomplishing it. If a university's department of business administration sets a goal of recruiting the best graduates of its bachelor's program into its MBA program, then that begins to generate ideas in the administrators and the faculty as to which means could be employed to enlist those students for the department. If a company has adopted the goal of becoming one of the three global market leaders for agricultural utility vehicles, it will use a so-called benchmarking process to compare itself with other companies in the business to find out whether even more appropriate means may exist for producing tractors.

In search logic, the saying "The end justifies the means" applies here (Luhmann 1973, 46). After all, the function of ends is to mobilize as much creative thinking as possible on the selection of suitable means. As a rule, however, the spectrum of means that can be utilized to achieve an end is always limited. When the management of a hydroelectric plant manufacturer announces the goal of capturing the markets in Greece or Turkey, then it is at least questionable whether bribery can be accepted as a legitimate means of achieving that goal.

In organizational science, this search for the best means of achieving a goal is referred to with the special term of *instrumental rationality*. This rationality does not refer to the selection of the goal. The goal has already been determined. Rather, it is a question of searching for suitable means to *achieve* the end. The goals of an organization may in themselves appear highly questionable to an observer, for example, the creation of prison camps for political dissidents, the training of suicide assassins, or the production of hairspray. Nevertheless, if an organization were to proceed as efficiently and effectively as possible in the selection of the means to reach its goals, it would deserve to be credited with a high degree of instrumental rationality. As the prominent sociologist Max Weber put it, acting in an instrumental-rational way first entails weighing various goals against one another, then selecting the most effective means of achieving the goals that have been defined, while taking the possibility of undesirable ancillary effects into consideration during the selection process (Weber 1976, 13). Classical strategy theory is firmly ensconced in the tradition of this instrumental-rational approach.

What position does strategy, when conceived in this way, occupy within a basic understanding of organizational structures?

1.2 Strategy as Part of Organizational Structure

According to Herbert A. Simon, organizational structures are decisions that serve as premises, that is, prerequisites, for other decisions (Simon 1957, 34ff.). Thus, organizational structures always involve the kind of decisions that are not exhausted in a single event, but influence a multitude of future decisions in the organization. When a maintenance worker decides to repair a malfunctioning machine on the shop floor, the decision would not qualify as a decision premise because its relevance applies only to this event. However, when the CEO decides that a member of the maintenance team must be on location within ten minutes to address all machine malfunctions in the production area, then that entails a decision premise (see Luhmann 1988, 172).

When examining decision premises, it makes sense to examine how they are positioned in relationship to three sides of the organization. In terms of the *formal side*, acceptance of the organization's expectations constitutes a condition of membership. You have to meet the officially formulated expectations, at least verbally, or risk your membership. But the formal side isn't everything. Many expectations are not set forth formally through a decision, but evolve only gradually. That constitutes the *informal side* of the organization. Finally, the organization also has a *display side*, which is the façade an organization creates for itself.

Following Herbert A. Simon, it has become accepted practice in organizational science to differentiate between three fundamentally different types of structure. The first type are the *decision programs*. To name some examples, these include goal systems, work instructions, IT programs, and policies. They determine which actions are to be viewed as right or wrong. The second type consists of *communication channels*. These include things like rules of operation, the division of labor, information channels, co-signing authority, hierarchical structure, or signature regulation. This determines the manner in which communication has to flow and which pathways it must follow. The third type of structures or decision premises can be understood as the *personnel*. The underlying idea is that it makes a difference for future decisions which person (or type of person) is chosen to fill a position (for greater detail see Luhmann 2000, 211ff.).

Programs—the first structure type—bundle the criteria that must be used in reaching decisions. They determine which actions are permitted, and which are not. In that respect, programs have the function of allowing the attribution of accountability when errors are made, thereby distributing blame in the organization. If an employee does not meet the goal of increasing revenues by ten percent, as specified by the program, they may try to find excuses, but ultimately the program allows the fault to be laid

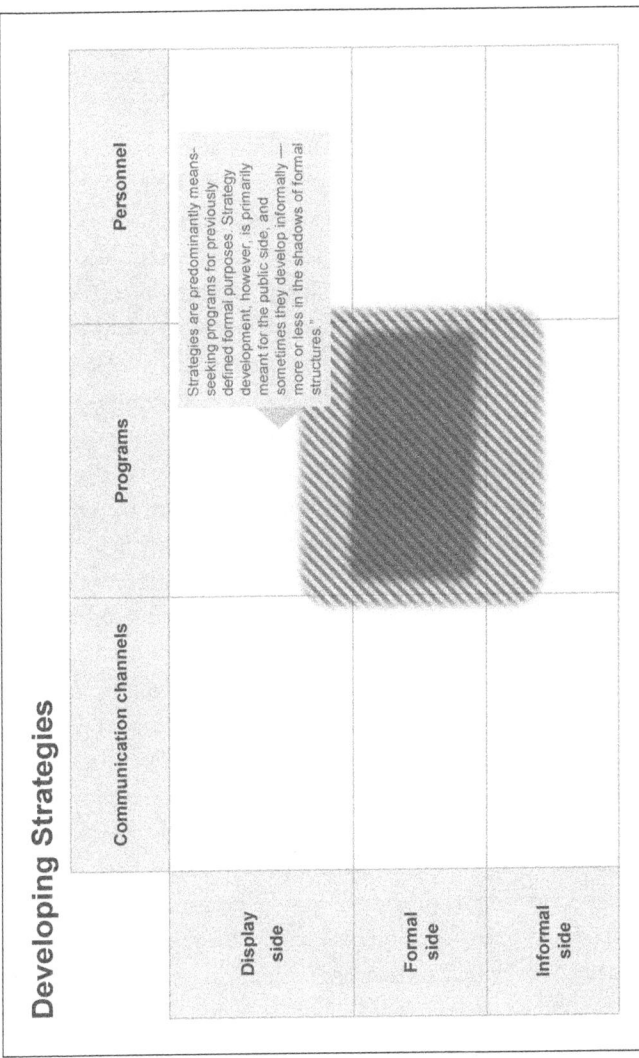

Diagram 1: Structure matrix for the analysis of organizations

primarily at their feet. In principle, there are two different kinds of programs: conditional programs and goal programs (for a concise summary see Luhmann 2000, 260ff.).

Conditional programs determine which actions must be undertaken when an organization registers a certain event. For example, when a pre-assembled component arrives at a workstation on an assembly line, then, according to a company-determined conditional program, a certain action must be initiated. If an unemployment office receives an application for unemployment benefits, the caseworker can use conditional programs that are specified by the agency and essentially regulated by law to determine precisely whether or not the circumstances warrant the payment of support. Consequently, in conditional programs there is a strong link between the prerequisite for an action (the *if*) and the execution of a decision (the *then*). The procedure is precisely defined. The program determines what must be done, and, in the case of conditional programs, what is not expressly permitted is forbidden.

Goal programs, on the other hand, determine which targets or objectives are to be achieved. Goal programming is found at the top of an organization, for example, when a company sets the goal of achieving the top position in the washing machine market. However, goal programming also takes place in the activities of middle and lower management when the so-called "management by objectives" approach is taken. But even simple activities can be governed by goal programs. In goal programs, the choice of means is left open. The objective is to reach the stated goal—no matter how—within certain limits. And this is the point where the concept of strategy enters. Ultimately, formulating a strategy describes the process of searching for suitable means to reach an objective; strategy implementation refers to the process of putting those means into effect once they have been identified as optimal.

Communication channels account for the second basic type of organizational decision premises. Initially, establishing legitimate points of contact, proper channels, and domains of responsibility massively limits the opportunities for communication. In reaching its decisions, the organization forgoes a large number of possible contacts as well as the participation of the entire range of potentially helpful and interested players. Only a limited number of legitimized contacts and authorized decision-makers are permitted, and the members must respect this if they do not wish to jeopardize their membership.

For the members of an organization, defined communication channels have an unburdening effect, as do all of the other types of structure. Those who are responsible for a certain decision may assume that it will be considered correct within the system and not be questioned. On the other hand, if a problem arises they must also assume responsibility for it and account for potential errors or the negative consequences of their decisions. This not only takes the onus off of managers who can assume that their subordinates will follow instructions, or at least officially act as if they were. It also takes the burden off of the subordinates, because they know with whom they may and may not speak (see Luhmann 2016, 90ff.). Well-defined communication channels also take pressure off the cooperative efforts between people at the same level, for example, because one department does not have to verify the correctness or usefulness of information received from another.

There are a wide variety of ways to regulate communications within an organization. The most prominent method of putting firm communication channels in place is certainly through a *hierarchy*. On the one hand, hierarchies define who is subordinate or superior to whom and therefore establish inequality. Yet at the same time they also produce equality because they specify which departments are situated on the same hierarchical level. A further important method of establishing communications channels is *co-signing authority.* Co-signing authority is based on the equality of rank among the participating organizational units. It is therefore correspondingly sensitive because there are no simple ways to resolve conflicts when they arise (see Luhmann 1988, 177). Another increasingly important way to define communication channels is to view them in terms of *project structures.* To this end, members of different departments are assembled to work on a project—which is to say, a goal program—over a specific period of time.

Hierarchies, co-signing authority, and project structures can be combined with one another to produce highly specific forms and networks of communication channels, for which very simplified terms are employed, such as a functional organization, divisional organization, or matrix organization. Depending on the combination of hierarchies, co-signing authority, and project structures chosen, there will be corresponding changes in the likelihood of cooperation, competition, or conflict in the organization. In the context of strategy processes, a high degree of creativity is mobilized to develop and implement such networked communications channels as a means of achieving a goal.

Whereas it is common practice in organizational science to classify programs and communication channels as organizational structures, the suggestion to view *personnel* as a third and coequal type of structure may be somewhat surprising. Personnel has been widely ignored in this context because of a blind spot that crept into organizational research via classical economics. Due to its orientation towards the classic ends-means model, managerial organizational research often views personnel merely as a means to an end, but not as something that represents a structure.

It will be clear to any observer, however, that organizations do not merely make decisions *about* personnel; personnel decisions also represent important premises for further decisions in the organization. In terms of future decisions, it makes a difference who occupies the position responsible for making them. Given the same position, a lawyer will often reach different decisions than an economist, who, in turn, will arrive at different decisions than a sociologist. People with upper-class socialization tend to reach different decisions than those from the lower social strata. It is also said that decision behavior among women tends to differ from men.

Organizations have different options when it comes to turning the personnel adjustment screw (Luhmann 1971, 208). The *hiring process* determines which type of person will make future decisions. The *firing* of individuals can be used to signal which kind of decisions the organization no longer wishes to have in the future. Particularly when positions at the highest levels are involved, this option is frequently used to send an internal and external message that different forms of decisions are to be expected. *Internal transfers* can be made in several directions: upward—in the form of a promotion, or to put someone on ice as a figurehead; downward—in the form of a demotion; or lateral. *Personnel development* represents an attempt to change people's behavior, so that while remaining in the same position they will reach different decisions in the future. Here, one often has the impression that personnel represent the organization's software, so to speak, and can be re-programmed in any way one desires through coaching and training seminars. In contrast, programs, technologies, and official procedures constitute the organization's hardware. Yet the opposite seems to be more plausible. Whereas an organization's plans and task descriptions can be "easily changed, practically with the stroke of a pen," people can only be "changed with difficulty, if at all" (Luhmann 2000, 280).

Having established this kind of understanding of organizational structure, we will recognize the position of strategies within the system. From a systems-theoretical point of view, communication channels, programs, and personnel are, in principle, equally ranking ways to structure organizations. Therefore, as a search for the means to accomplish a previously defined goal program, strategies are ultimately only one possible form of organizational structure.

THEORY

The Strengths of a Systems-Theoretical Definition of Strategy

It is understandable that such a precise attempt at defining strategy has drawn a significant amount of criticism. The trend within the strategy debate is to establish an eclectic theory that can accommodate very different paradigms. For those who advocate a narrow definition of the concept of strategy, the burden of proof is high. They must explain how their definition relates to the other definitions of strategy and demonstrate why it is superior. They must furnish proof not only that the relevant discussions of strategy can be replicated with the help of their definition, but also that integrating it leads to a better understanding of the discussions. They must delineate what kind of new scientific approaches will be opened up for the understanding of strategy. Not least, because of the practical implications typical for the discussion of strategy, they have to demonstrate what defining strategy with the help of the end-means model represents for the practice of developing strategies.

The Resolution of the Artificial Contradiction Between Strategy and Structure

An initial benefit of a narrow definition of strategy is that it helps to resolve the controversy over the relationship between strategy and structure in the Hegelian sense, or, in other words, to overcome the contradiction of two concepts, while at the same time preserving the distinction between them and ultimately synthesizing them at a higher level. Ever since the first studies claiming to be scientific were written on strategy in the 1960s, a contentious debate has been carried on as to whether the formation of organizational structure follows from managerial strategy decisions or if, conversely, strategy decisions are direct results of the structure of the organization.

Under the label of "structure follows strategy," Alfred Chandler (1962), a forefather of the discussion of strategy in management, promulgated the idea that organizations respond to changes in environmental conditions by adjusting their strategies, and that their structures are subsequently adapted to the strategies. In contrast to Chandler, David Hall and Maurice A. Saias (1980) used the catchy formula "strategy follows structure" to point out that strategies are instead the outcome of an organization's structure. According to Hall and Saias, information about the environment can only be processed through a lens that has been created by the structure of the organization itself. In their opinion, the strategy process can only result from the structure of the organization.

There have been a multitude of research papers published on the subject of this comparatively simple juxtaposition, claiming to demonstrate the degree to which strategy decisions shape the structure of an organization or, conversely, the extent to which structure influences strategies. Rather than simply contrasting structure and strategy, it became popular to assume recursive relationships between the two. A strategy, the assumption ran, influenced the structure of an organization, which, in turn, had an impact on the formulation of a strategy, which then influenced the structure of the organization (for examples, see Mintzberg 1990b, 171ff.; Amburgey/Dacin 1994, 1427ff.).

While the recursive explanatory model is certainly not wrong, it suffers from the fact that it, too, does not specify what structure and strategies are actually supposed to be, or how they relate to one another. The debate over whether "structure follows strategy" or "strategy follows structure," as well as the formula of "structure follows strategy and strategy follows structure," are misleading because they treat the concepts of strategy and structure as coequal. If strategy is the process through which the means to achieve an end are sought and implemented, then strategy can be nothing other than an aspect of organizational structure. If one wishes to express this in the language of the controversy, one would have to say that "strategy *is* structure" or, more precisely, "strategy is *part* of the structure."

Such specification now puts us in a far better position to describe the relationship between decisions about goal programs and the choice of means to attain the goals, and other structural decisions. When decisions about the structure of organizations are involved, there is always the possibility that one of the structure types will "take the lead." It can happen that hierarchical communication channels are viewed as fixed, and an attempt is undertaken to formulate program and personnel requirements for the existing departments. Yet it may also come to pass that the structural decisions are conceived in terms of goal programs, in other words, an attempt is undertaken to find suitable communication channels and the appropriate personnel for goals that have already been set. Particularly when personnel as a decision premise is immobile, it is beneficial for the organization to define suitable programs and appropriate communication channels.

Instead of always considering an organization through the lens of its goal program, as in classical approaches to strategy, the objective now becomes to reconstruct for each individual organization which structure type is taking the lead and for what reason. In isolated cases, the reason can be attributed to thinking in terms of goal programs, although it can also happen that an organization is conceived under the personnel aspect, or that the communication channels, which are viewed as immutable, are used as a starting point for a process of change.

The Resolution of the Relationship Between End and Means

Alfred Chandler's definitions of strategies contain an ambiguity which is actually fertile in the sense that it allows us to define the concept of strategy in greater detail by drawing on systems theory. Chandler (1962, 14) defines strategy as "the determination of the long-term goals and objectives of an enterprise, and the adoption of courses of action and the allocation of resources necessary for carrying out these goals." In his eyes, therefore, strategy represents both the definition of goals as well as the determination of the means to fulfill them.

This dual definition has led to confusion in the discussion of strategy. Sometimes the concept of strategy tends to be used to emphasize the formulation of a goal program. This leads to statements such as "the company's strategy is to increase revenues by two percent this year." In other formulations, meanwhile, the concept of strategy tends to underscore the choice of resources. In that case, the wording reflects that the objective of a strategy process is to "identify the appropriate means to increase revenue by two percent this year." Sometimes the job of strategies is seen as establishing goals *and* making decisions about resources (see Schendel/Hofer 1979, 15ff.).

According to Henry Mintzberg, Bruce Ahlstrand, and Joseph Lampel (2005), there is considerable confusion about strategies. For a deeper understanding of strategies, it is problematic if the concept is used, arbitrarily, in one instance for the formulation of goals, in another for the identification of resources, and in yet a third to indicate both. The cause of the confusion is to be found in the early phase of strategy research, when opinions were expressed off the cuff, as it were, without systematically referencing the discussion in organizational research over end-means relationships, which, in turn, followed from Max Weber.

From the perspective of systems theory, the relationship between ends and means becomes clear when we focus on a distinctive feature of organizations, namely, that, as a rule, end-means chains are formed. In a business or a public administration, it is not simply that a goal is defined for which various resources are then sought. Rather, when a means that appears to be suitable has been identified, it is itself treated as a (sub)goal for which, in turn, suitable means are sought. Subsequently, the latter means are treated as a goal, and a search for suitable means to achieve this (sub-sub)goal is initiated.

It now becomes clear why sometimes in strategy processes the goal identification aspect receives emphasis, and sometimes the search for means. For example, if management decides that the rejection rate in the production process has to be cut from one percent to 0.5 percent, then, from an executive perspective, that is a means—a strategy—to reach the goal of reducing costs. From the perspective of the production manager who has been instructed to reach this quality target, it presents itself as a goal for which he must develop the appropriate means, which is to say, strategies. In the strategy process, the question of whether something is seen as an end or a means is substantially determined by one's position in the organization.

The Clarification of the Relationship Between Plan and Reality

One criticism that has been raised against the discussion of strategy is that it focuses too much on strategy in the sense of planning considerations and not enough on strategy as concrete work or, as it is now referred to, "strategizing." Inspired by the "practical turn" in the social sciences, the focus shifted to how the "practitioners" of strategies, and underutilization of "practices" such as workflow rules or tools, create concrete "practice" (see Whittington 1996; Whittington 2003; Whittington 2006, or Jarzabkowski et al. 2007). An important contribution of this strategy-as-practice approach has been to initiate more realistic and richly detailed descriptions of strategic practices in organizations.

Nevertheless, this very approach of strategy as practice raises the question of the relationship between strategic practices and strategic plans. Since the praxeological perspective focuses primarily on what people "do" in strategy processes, this is the point where it comes up against its limitations (Cloutier/Whittington 2013, 803). Much as in the classical subject and actor theories in sociology, the practical actions taken are placed at the center of attention, thereby obscuring the relationship between plan and practice (however, see Seidl 2007). Systems theory allows us to address the relationship between plan and practice because the concept of structure is not built on the regularity of actions but rather on expectations (see Hendry/Seidl 2003). Structures, according to Niklas Luhmann (1984, 362ff.), represent expectations that do not determine actions but rather burden those who deviate from the expectations with the obligation to explain why they have done so. And it is precisely this perspective that puts systems theory in a position to observe the difference between expectations in the form of formalized programs and concrete practices in organizations.

The Position of Strategy Processes within Organizations as a Whole

In the literature on strategy, a lot of creative energy is expended on defining strategies merely as a search for the means to accomplish a certain type of goal program. For example, the case is made for not defining strategy as the search for the means to achieve an organization's overall goal (for example, maximizing profit in businesses), but rather to limit the concept of strategy to the search for resources to accomplish more strongly operationalized goal programs (on this discussion see Hofer/Schendel 1978, 18f.). Hierarchies of goal programs are created to position strategies between the goal programs of the organization's objectives or even its mission on the one hand, and its policies and programs on the other (Hunger/Wheelen 1996, 10).

The idea is not to use the concept of strategy for the search for means to accomplish goal programs as a matter of principle, but to apply it only for the search for means to achieve special forms of goal programs. An expression of this can be seen in the fact that strategies are always mentioned when the goals of an organization are "fundamental" or when the search for resources involves "long-term" goals.

Yet organizations harbor a multitude of goal programs. The target of attaining market leadership in Eastern Europe for drill sets is just as much a goal program as when an executive instructs her assistant to serve her a latte macchiato prepared with hand-foamed milk at the beginning of the workday. Targeting an annual return on investment of 15 percent is every bit as much a goal program that mobilizes a search for resources as the order issued to a Mafia debt collector to exact weekly protection money from restaurants in a certain part of town. Now, does it make sense to apply the concept of strategy to the search for resources to achieve such widely differing goal programs?

Nevertheless, the criteria are not clear as to why the search for the means to accomplish a goal program is referred to as a search for strategy in one case but not in another. The attempt to chase down a latte macchiato—even in a remote region—may not deserve to be designated as a strategy from the perspective of the caffeine-craving executive, but it could very well appear as a strategic project to the executive assistant charged with the task. If one assumes that strategies are defined not only at the top of an organization for the purpose of achieving major goals, but are defined throughout the organization, then there is no reason to reserve the concept of strategy for specific cases of searching for means in organizations.

The Explanation for the Narrow Focus on Businesses

It is striking that the discussion of strategy focuses so heavily on businesses. The notion that a company requires a separate strategy department was first formulated in enterprises, and most of the strategy tools that consultants have developed are aimed at positioning companies in their market environment. The leading research studies have been conducted on strategy development processes in businesses, and the fact that the majority of foundational scientific publications on strategy focus narrowly on businesses is an indication of how difficult it is to conceive of strategies in connection with other types of organizations such as hospitals, administrative bodies, or political parties.

From the perspective of systems theory, this requires an explanation because there is no reason to consider companies more important or significant than other types of organizations.

Granted, the economy of modern society is inconceivable without businesses. Yet by the same token one can just as little imagine education without schools, science without universities and research institutes, politics without administrations, or religions without organized denominations.

One explanation for the concentrated focus of the strategy discussion on businesses could be that corporations have played a pioneering role in many questions of reorganization. Additionally, one could point out that, because of their ties to markets, businesses tend to be more dependent on rapid changes in their environment than government agencies or schools. Furthermore, we need only mention that businesses, as a rule, are willing to pay higher consulting fees than agencies or universities and that, consequently, consulting firms gear their tools primarily to commercial enterprises.

Yet if one views strategy as a search to identify the resources to meet previously defined goals, this theoretical position opens up a further reason why the strategy discussion is so focused on business. To a greater degree than other types of organizations, businesses are shaped by the end-means model.

Admittedly, goal programs can also be found in public administrations, law enforcement agencies, or the courts, but under the rule of law, in any case, such organizations are structured primarily by conditional programs. If the police did not adhere to conditional programs in the form of laws, behaving instead in accordance with abstract objectives such as the prevention of unrest, countries would turn into police states. An agency that did not abide by the conditional programs set forth in the administrative regulations would suffer from a legitimacy deficit (for greater detail, see Luhmann 1973, 88ff.). This focus on conditional programs can explain why such types of organizations are not as receptive as businesses when it comes to a strategy discussion that is geared to the search for suitable resources.

Now, one might object that over the last several decades, strategy discussions have also taken place in administrative bodies, law enforcement agencies, hospitals, schools, and universities. This, too, can be understood in terms of the narrow definition of strategy as a search for resources to fulfill a goal program. While there has been no change in the fundamental constraint by conditional programs in many types of organizations, catchwords such as "new public management" have allowed a greater orientation toward goal programs to arise in administrative bodies, law enforcement agencies, and universities, thereby almost automatically opening the gates for discussions of "strategic positioning."

2.
The Lure and Limitations of an Instrumental-Rational Approach

In the classical understanding of strategy, a strategy process begins with the specification of a mission or a long-term goal for an organization. The next step is to determine the various means necessary to accomplish the overarching goal, based on an analysis of the organization's environment, its internal capacities, and the available resources. Then the various strategy alternatives are analyzed in detail with respect to their potential and risks, and the strategy that guarantees the accomplishment of the overarching, long-term goal is selected. Next, the chosen strategy is operationalized. Quantitative targets are formulated, milestones defined, and action plans prepared. Management monitors progress at regular intervals (for examples of this approach see Hussey 1998, 71; for a concise presentation, see Mintzberg 1994, 36ff.).

2.1 A Portrayal of Standard Procedure

This classical understanding of strategy is advocated by the so-called Design School or the Planning School and reflects an understanding of organizations that organizational scholars call *goal fetishism*. The organization is seen as revolving from A to Z around its top-level goal. The organization's leadership sets an overarching goal, and then the resources needed to reach the ultimate goal are defined. The means that have been thus defined are then identified as subgoals, and, in turn, resources must be sought to achieve them. This process creates a pyramid-shaped concatenation of superordinate and subordinate goals that allows every action within the organization to be examined for its utility. In short, what this entails is the structure of a "strategy-focused organization" (Kaplan/Norton 2001, 2ff.).

The organizational reasoning behind this end-means thinking has existed for a long time. As early as 1932, Fritz Nordsieck, a founder of the discipline of business economics in Germany, expressed the view that the task an organization had to fulfill should be the "point of departure" for defining the organization's structure (Nordsieck 1932, 10). According to Nordsieck, an analysis of the organization was to systematically break down the overall task into subtasks, and the subtasks were to be assigned to specific units of the organization or, better yet, to specific positions. The meshing that occurred during the fulfillment of the subtasks would then result in the accomplishment of the overarching objective.

This concept is predicated on the idea that the strategy process does not contain contradictory goals or subgoals. If goals or subgoals were to conflict with one another, then fulfilling the subtasks would not result in the completion of the overarching task. The contradictions would already create confusion while a strategy was under development and ultimately prevent it from being articulated coherently.

The instrumental-rational approach draws a strict distinction between the development of a strategy and its implementation.

According to this line of thinking, a strategy must first be properly and completely formulated before one can begin to think about putting it into practice. This idea calls to mind the military strategist who confers with his staff to devise a strategy and then passes it on, in the form of an order, to the soldiers on the front. After that, the execution of the orders is ensured through military discipline and is therefore comparatively unproblematic (on this analogy, see Whittington 1993, 17).

This method often finds expression in strategic master plans that run several hundred pages and lay out precisely defined targets, schedules, and budget allocations. The master plan includes detailed descriptions of subgoals, all of which are supposedly "smart," in other words, specific, measurable, accepted, realistic, and time-based (see Doran 1981). The timetables sometimes state to the day, and not infrequently even to the exact hour, when hundreds of these individual subgoals are to be achieved. And the budget for achieving each of the subgoals is then precisely set in dollars, euros, or renminbi. Then, all that remains is for the plans to be made accessible to the relevant employees and for management to monitor employee compliance (see Goold/Campbell 1987, 74f.).

2.2 On the Popularity of an Instrumental-Rational Approach to the Strategy Discussion

The reason for the popularity of the strategy discussion in practice lies in its instrumental-rational orientation. In the early 1960s, management author Peter F. Drucker had planned to title on his books "Business Strategies." The publisher consulted with executives, though, and found that they could not relate to the concept of strategy. The book was accordingly renamed *Managing for Results* (Drucker 1964) Only a short time thereafter, however, strategy became the "new thing." After that, if a consulting firm wanted to approach top-level management, they no longer saw their job as providing support for day-to-day business operations; instead, they believed their main task was to assist organizations with their strategic reorientations (see Stewart 2009, 152f.).

From this instrumental-rational perspective, the task of application-oriented science—following as comprehensive a compilation of information as possible and the careful weighing of alternatives—consists of whispering more suitable resources for reaching the overall goal into management's ear. Science is believed to be primarily a method for producing conclusive knowledge that can be directly applied by management (Whitley 1984, 369f.). The result has been the creation of a tight network of corporations, consulting firms, and business schools with a host of professors of strategy who—to quote a wry observation by Matthew Stewart (2009, 218)—earn their money by providing consulting services to companies and then recounting the stories of their successes in articles and books with a light scholarly touch.

In the meantime, the discussion about orientating organizations has become dominated by a specialized "strategy industry" (see David 2012). Every self-respecting consulting firm or professor of strategy now develops his own strategy tools. In the beginning, the relatively simple four-field models were created. SWOT analysis promised to capture an organization's Strengths,

Weaknesses, Opportunities, and Threats. If market cultivation strategies were involved, the Product/Market Grid was supposed to permit differentiation between market penetration, market development, product development, and diversification. The Growth Share Matrix or the BCG Matrix distinguished between types of potential for every product, designating them as dogs, problem children, cows, or stars. This phase was followed by more complex models that expected managers to think in five or even seven dimensions. The Five Forces were introduced, which make the success of a business dependent on the strength of its competitors in the field, the bargaining capabilities of its suppliers and buyers, and the threats posed by new market participants or substitute products. The 7S Framework demanded that an organization's orientation take Strategy, Structure, Systems, Skills, Staff, Style, and Shared Values into account.

The charm of these tools is that they easily connect with businesses, administrations, or hospitals. Since they are easy to learn, can be taught and tested in MBA coursework, disseminated in management journals, and introduced at conferences for executives, there is generally no difficulty in gaining acceptance for such tools during change processes. When someone says that the first step is to conduct Stakeholder Mapping, a SWOT Analysis, or create a Product/Market Grid, this creates a basis for communication in the company because most people believe that they understand what lies concealed behind these proven methods. In this sense, the tools fulfill an important function in producing connectivity in an organization.

Initially, the implication of these methods is convincing: if one only had "solid information about market trends and global developments"; if one only had insight into the business processes and "knowledge about optimization potentials"; if one possessed "an overview of the sector, its difficulties and best-practice models"; if "proven tools to develop structured solutions were available" and one engaged "highly qualified consultants" with "pronounced analytical skills" then—according to this line of thinking—nothing could happen to the organization. But unfortunately, the situation is more complicated.

2.3 The Limitations of an Instrumental-Rational Approach

Complaints about the "implementation gap" clearly indicate that classical strategy management has its limitations. Some argue that organizations do not so much lack good visions, ideas, or strategies, as much as the corresponding abilities to realize them. Some lament the fact that while organizations have little difficulty creating plans, they lack "implementation excellence," the ability to swiftly put their plans into action in practical terms.

In the classical approaches to strategy management, the implementation gap is not taken as a reason to reconsider methods for developing strategies. Instead, organizations are called upon to develop greater implementation competence. This suggests that there is no need to change anything in the instrumental-rational approach; one simply has to place management under obligation to implement the adopted strategies through the use of professional project management. This position does not require executives, consultants, and professors to change their strategy development methods, while at the same time it allows them to open up "implementation management" as a new field of activity.

There is a different explanation for the implementation gap that we consider more plausible. The implementation gap following a strategy process should not be attributed to a lack of commitment at top management levels, a lack of professionalism in implementation management at the middle management level, or inferior consultants. Rather, it is the unavoidable result of an instrumental-rational perspective during the strategy process. In organizational research, there is now broad consensus that the notion of organizations as harmonious derivations of subgoals from a distributed superordinate goal is nothing more than a figment of the imagination among senior executives. On the contrary, organizations are characterized by competing goals, regularly occurring end-means reversals, goals as pure window dressing, arbitrary and unnoticed goal switching, and by subgoals taking on a life of their own. In the development of strategies, this must not be understood as organizational pathology; instead, the method of developing strategies must be adapted to such characteristics.

Developing Strategies when Goals Conflict

Organizations often endorse a whole array of goals, thereby implying that the ends are compatible with, or even support, one another. As an example, some companies define their goals in terms of having profitable business operations, tapping new markets, developing fundamentally innovative products, treating their employees extremely well, and additionally serving their community (Kühl 2013, 53f.).

As soon as the goals are operationalized, however, it becomes clear that they generally conflict with one another. The development of new innovative products lowers profit in the short term and thereby reduces the firm's ability to pay higher dividends, wages, or taxes. Raising the dividend for shareholders can often only be achieved by decreasing investment in the development of new products, cutting salaries, or reducing tax payments (see Luhmann 1981, 405).

Classical strategy management admits that such goal conflicts exist, but then advocates solving them through "conscious prioritization." According to this line of reasoning, "weighting" can be used to produce "goal rankings." The prioritization assigns "greater weight to specific goals" so that goal conflicts can be defused. In the end, the dominant idea is that if there are conflicting "multiple objectives" in an organization, rational decisions can be reached with the help of "goal weighting." Thus, confronted with the organizational reality of goal conflicts, the normative model of an organization consisting of unequivocal "goal rankings" is not abandoned but actually receives additional emphasis.

From the perspective of systems-theoretical organizational research, one cannot dispute that there are successful attempts at forming "goal rankings." Yet according to Luhmann, if the entire organization were structured according to this notion, it would focus the organization "on a much too simple view of its environment." "Down to the technical details of its work, a bias would be imposed on the organization" with respect to the simplicity of its environment. As a result, "numerous problems would have to be glossed over and some experiences created through collaboration would not be gained or could at least not be discussed" (Luhmann 1973, 76).

For these reasons, the reality of organizations is often more complex than the end-means models of classical strategy processes suggests. Organizations can withstand goal conflict for decades and derive their autonomy from precisely this source. One need only think of universities with their goal conflict between teaching and research, or the goal conflict in prisons between re-socializing inmates and the need to keep them in custody for security purposes. Or, in addition to their dominant formal goals, organizations develop informal ones that enable them to react to the complexity of their environment.

Strategy Development as Legitimation: Goals as Window Dressing for the External World

One form of criticism directed at strategy formulations is that they are too vague. According to Richard Rumelt (2011, 34ff.), for example, the sign of a "bad strategy" is that the goals are fuzzy. In his view, this often results when people from different departments and units attempt to assert their interests during a planning meeting. Frequently, the outcome is either a wish list with a multitude of possible strategies, or formulaic compromises that are so abstract that everyone can agree with them. While it is correct to describe such abstract formulations as the result of strategy processes, the fact is overlooked that they, too, have a function in the organization.

As Niklas Luhmann recognized early on, not all goals are so instructive that they allow us to deduce the right, let alone the *only* right means to achieve them (see Luhmann 1973, 94). Slogans such as "the customer is king," the "humanization of the workplace," "profit maximization," or "environmental protection" represent abstract behavioral expectations at best. The question of which behaviors are expected in a concrete situation is left unaddressed. If we are simply told, "Simultaneously maximize everything that's good," we will have difficulty inferring instructions for handling specific situations. How far should we take the idea of "protecting our environment?" Would it also be permissible to kill somebody in an emergency? What are we expected to do if our actions line up with "the customer is king," but they hurt employees, the "company's most important capital resource" (Kühl 2013, 54)?

The formulation of somewhat abstract goals—one might also call them *values*—is often not at all intended to serve as a set of instructions for concrete actions but aims instead at gaining acceptance of the organization in its surroundings (see Luhmann 1964a, 108ff.). If business executives in a capitalist economy do not aggressively affirm the goal of profit maximization, they will presumably raise the hackles of their shareholders, just as a labor union official will run afoul of labor activists if she does not strive to accomplish the objective of representing union members as effectively as possible, or at least communicate that she is doing so.

As a result, organizations often turn into veritable "affirmation machines," regularly embracing every conceivable social value that is *en vogue*. In the meantime, not only businesses but also hospitals, universities, schools, public administrations, the military, law enforcement agencies, and associations pledge their commitment to extensive catalogs of values. Although these values have a "high consensus potential" (see Luhmann 1972, 88f.) because they are so abstract, they contradict all of the demands that are classically placed on strategies.

Nevertheless, as Henry Mintzberg (1990b, 184), among others, has pointed out, abstract formulations in the form of strategies have their advantages. Granted, the more clearly a strategy is expressed and formalized, the more firmly it will anchor itself in the thinking of the members of the organization and the more difficult it will become to deviate from it. If an organization works primarily with abstract value formulations that are subject to interpretation, it can adapt to concrete changes more quickly.

Unplanned Goal Changes

Strategy changes often transpire unnoticed by customers, employees, or suppliers and occasionally even by those at the top levels of the organization (see Inkpen/Choudhury 1995). For this reason, Henry Mintzberg and James A. Waters differentiate between "intended strategies" and "emergent strategies" (Mintzberg/Waters 1985). From a systems-theoretical perspective, one would speak of intended strategies as organizational decision premises that have already been determined, or, more precisely, of the means that have been decided upon for a previously defined goal program. Emergent strategies, on the other hand, would be seen as decision premises that are not the subject of a decision, that is, as decision premises that have segregated out from a multitude of decisions without a prior formal decision having been reached about them.

This observation of the interplay between intended and emergent strategies affords revealing insight into development processes in organizations. At a first, superficial glance, we might characterize McDonald's as a chain of fast food stores with the goal of selling hamburgers, French fries, and warm and cold caffeinated beverages as profitably as possible. In reality, McDonald's qualifies as one of the world's largest real estate lessors, with property holdings valued in excess of thirty billion dollars. The company's business model is based on making a piece of real estate available to small business owners and then turning a profit on them, not only by collecting fees for the use of the McDonald's logo and selling them frozen ground meat patties, but primarily by charging them handsome rents and leasing fees. Harry J. Sonneborn, who was the grey eminence behind McDonald's chairman Ray Croc in the early days, once expressed it succinctly in a statement intended for banks. McDonald's, he said, was first and foremost a player in the real estate sector, not the fast food industry (see Kühl 2013, 56).

Naturally, organizations do not enjoy unlimited freedom to change their goals, if only because companies, public administrations, or hospitals have invested large sums of money to purchase machinery, provide training and professional development for their staff, or develop procedures; in other words, they have invested in things that cannot be readily retooled for a different organizational goal. It may be possible to beat swords into plowshares, but not into computers. With some effort, engineers can be retrained as call-center workers, but they can't be transformed into an elite combat unit. In this context, economists speak of "sunk costs"—resources that have already been spent on certain things and are simply no longer available for other purposes. Nonetheless, in spite of the commitments that organizations have entered through previous decisions, the speed at which they revamp their goals is fascinating (Kühl 2013, 55f.).

Reversing the End and the Means

The discussion of core competencies in the strategy debate has drawn attention to an important aspect of this issue: organizations are not entirely free in the choice of their goals, but they are strongly dependent on the resources at their disposal. The available resources that enable an organization to attain its goal better than its competitors are understood as its core competencies (Prahalad/Hamel 1990). These considerations stem from a resource-based approach developed by Jeffrey Pfeffer and Gerald R. Salancik (1978), according to which an organization is understood primarily in terms of the skills and abilities at its disposal. Core competencies can be understood as the resources that ensure an organization's survival, as its competitors cannot readily duplicate them, or they might provide quick access to new products.

This brings us to an important point. Means do not only serve to achieve the goal of an organization. In practice, means often take on a quality of their own that no longer has anything to do with the original goal. The end for which the means were originally developed is forgotten, and the means themselves are retained with such enthusiasm that one might think *they* are now the organization's goal. In education, school testing no longer functions merely as a way to monitor learning progress; tests have instead become the very reason for, and focus of, learning. Eventually, getting together in church-sponsored youth groups, at senior citizen meetings in the parish hall, and gathering for coffee after church no longer amounts to praising the Lord in the sense of "where two or three are gathered together in my name." Instead, the primary focus of parish work has now shifted to socializing (Kühl 2013, 59f.).

The problem with the concept of core competencies is that the observation that many goals are defined solely on the basis of available resources (which is convincing from a systems-theoretical perspective) is equated too quickly with an instrumental-rational understanding of organizations. When core competencies are understood as a "harmonious association of resources and abilities" with which "a firm can stand out in the market" (Schilling 2013, 117), then we are acting as if an organization used a strategy process to clarify which resources it has at its disposal and then derived corresponding goals. Although such planned searches for goals to suit the available means do exist, these processes generally tend to be unplanned.

As a rule, end-means reversals happen incrementally, so that the organization barely notices. In the university context, raising additional funds was long viewed strictly as a means of financing expensive research. It would never have occurred to anyone to confuse raising sums of money for research with the actual execution of the research. Yet due to the search for quantifiable measures of successful research, attracting financial support has in many cases transformed from a means to an end. Even fundraising for a major project, research in a particular area, or for a cluster of researchers is now viewed as an indication of scientific excellence in its own right, well before the scientists deliver their results. Accordingly, questions about the amount of funding secured—"How many millions have you generated in research funding?"—often appear to play a more important role in the application for a professorship than the actual quality of the candidate's publications.

EXAMPLE

End-Means Shifts in the Strategy Process

A well-known, long-term study of the Intel Corporation by Robert A. Burgelman (1994) provides an illustrative example of how a shift in means can lead to a gradual change of goals. Drawing on his observations and documentation, Burgelman reconstructs how the computer technology firm transformed itself between 1985 and 1996 from a producer of its innovative DRAM memory chips into a manufacturer of microprocessors. The primary purpose of the analysis was to point out and explain shifts in strategy. However, reinterpreting the study according to the end-means model described above also allows us to conclude that it was a change in resources that led to the reorientation of Intel's goals.

During the company's founding phase around 1968, Intel was focused on the development, and, beginning in 1970, the sale of DRAM memory chip technology. This product allowed the company to supplant the magnetic core memory technology prevalent at the time. After successfully entering the market, it took Intel only four years to capture global market leadership in memory chips. Yet the success of the company's technology soon inspired imitators who began offering similar mass-produced chips in the market at a better price. In order to retain its market position, Intel initially pinned its hopes on developing and manufacturing new, higher performance products. As the competitive environment in the global market shifted from innovation to mass-market production, however, Intel was forced out of its market leadership position beginning in 1974. By 1980, its global market share had declined to roughly three percent (see Burgelman/Grove 1996).

The loss of market share notwithstanding, the goal of the company's strategy decisions up until 1985 aimed at retaining DRAM production as the firm's core competence. Yet in addition to DRAM chip technology, Intel had launched two other products in the market: microprocessors and EPROMs. Both of them were simply spinoffs from DRAM research. While microprocessors were initially viewed only as a means of increasing revenues, by 1985 they had ousted DRAMs from Intel's production program, even though the company's official strategy until 1985 remained focused on the production of DRAMs as its core product.

This development was the result of planning which stipulated that the production of the DRAMs, EPROMs, and microprocessors—all manufactured in the same factories—should be organized according to their respective margins. Microprocessors proved to be the most profitable of the three products. Contrary to the strategy decisions from top management, middle management increasingly utilized manufacturing capacity for the production of microprocessors, and little by little the production of DRAMs was cut back.

Since 1982, middle management had been suggesting a separate production facility specifically for DRAMs. Top management was initially opposed to the idea, not least because it feared the company would suffer a loss of image and identity. Only in 1984, when the company faced a decision about whether to invest in a large-scale plant that would lower the unit cost of producing DRAMs, did Intel choose to exit the market. Beginning in October 1985, strategic decisions focused exclusively on the production of microprocessors. Middle management's insistence on the production strategy they had implemented ultimately led to a goal change that affected the entire organization (case study is based on the report in Radtke 2015).

Goals are Dependent on Local Rationalities

The idea that organizations can be broken down into end-means relationships becomes questionable in light of the fact that the various organizational units develop their own targets and goals. The reasons for this lie in their orientation toward different segments of the environment and in the differences in goal orientations resulting from the division of labor. Each individual unit justifies its local targets and goals rhetorically by citing the organization's overarching goal. But since each unit of the organization views its own local perspective as absolute, it becomes impossible to merge the different local rationalities into a harmonious, coordinated concept (Cyert/March 1992, 165).

For strategy processes, this means that there is no all-encompassing view of the organization. The CEO, the board or the strategy team cannot claim to have the "proper" perspective on the organization. Instead, each of their perspectives represents only one of the many that are produced. When developing a strategy, one encounters the widely divergent scripts, models, and ways of thinking of the various units. During the strategy development process, these elements frequently collide with force.

In the struggle, a great variety of forms of influence are exerted, often simultaneously. There is a possibility that the dispute will lead to an agreement about the course of action going forward. The perspectives of individual units can shift because the strategy process allows them to gain insight into the ways of thinking, reasoning, and rationalities of other units. Yet attempts are always made to exert power and enlist others for one's own favored course of action. There are also processes based on trust, however, where, without closer examination, individuals or groups are allowed to try out something new in the hope that they, in turn, will provide blind support someday when they try something risky themselves.

From this perspective, a strategy is a possible orientation about which various groups within the organization have agreed on. Here, Henry Mintzberg (1978, 945) speaks of an "emergent strategy" that forms through controversy between various groups in the organization and is not the result of a high-level decision. As stated so incisively by Richard Whittington (1993, 24), strategies are always the product of a "political compromise," not a "profit maximizing calculation."

Goals Are Sought after the Fact

Research on organizational decision processes has further radicalized criticism of the instrumental-rational model. A company, public administration, or university will portray its decision-making processes to the outside world as if defining goals came first—through elaborate strategy processes, goal setting workshops, or by virtue of a lone decision by the CEO—and all subsequent decisions were geared to achieving the goals. The suggestion is that goals and purposes come first, and then the actions.

While such cases no doubt occur, many times strategy becomes explicit only *after* action has been taken and the effects of the action have been observed. When Henry Mintzberg (1990a, 105ff.) defines strategy as a "pattern in a stream of action," he then points out that such patterns are only discernible after they have happened. Gary Hamel (1998, 10) underscores this point when he emphasizes that the "strategy industry"—the strategy consulting firms, business school professors, the planners in the organizations, and the authors of management books—always recognize strategies only after a development has proven successful. While the post hoc explanations produced for an organization's success may be breathtakingly beautiful, no one would have dared predict success beforehand. But instead of proclaiming a search for the "secrets of strategy development," the idea is to investigate whether it is the norm that strategies can only be reconstructed after the fact (Kühl 2013, 61f.).

A large body of research on organizational decision-making shows that organizations are constantly making decisions without always being clear about the basis or reason for them. Once a decision has produced an effect, the search begins for potential goals that might serve as justification for the decision. According to James G. March, organizational decision-making behavior involves not only the goal-oriented activity of the members, but also a continual process of finding goals to legitimize activities that have already occurred. In brief, "the action often precedes the goal" and "announcement of the goal is then often a justification of steps that have already been taken" (March 1976, 72).

Examples of such post hoc goal definitions can be observed in consulting projects where goals emerge only slowly. Companies, government agencies, and hospitals use tender documents and consulting contracts as a means of suggesting that they have a clear idea—even *before* they award the job—of the goals they want to reach through the consultants' efforts. And some projects do adhere to the goals initially agreed upon. If the consultants' work produces unexpected effects, however, then goals must be sought to legitimize them after the fact. In the end, the purpose of the consulting project is reported to have been, say, to identify the need for further continuing education offerings, whereas the project was initially discussed within the context of performance-based compensation models.

EXAMPLE

The Unintended Invention of Polyethylene

One example of the way goals are defined after the fact and thereby justify the actions that preceded them is the discovery of polyethylene, the material from which plastic bags are made (for greater detail, see Allen 1967). In 1933, there was an explosion in a laboratory belonging to Imperial Chemical Industries (ICI). It resulted in the creation of a new material, but since there was a risk of a second explosion, closer investigation of the material was prohibited (Whittington 1993, 87).

Due to certain changes in the structure of the organization, the material that the explosion had accidentally created was in danger of being forgotten. Because of the explosion, steps were taken beginning in 1933 to upgrade the technical capabilities of the laboratory and to improve operating safety. In addition, the Dyestuffs Committee, which had previously supported ad hoc research on chemical experiments entailing high pressure, decided to withdraw its funding support. This led to the disbanding of the team that had been collaborating when the strange substance was produced. At that moment, there was nothing to indicate the later significance of polyethylene.

In 1935, a company researcher who had heard of the accident decided to repeat the experiment under controlled circumstances, although without backing from a higher level. The first attempt was made during the evening hours of December 19,

1935, although no protocol was recorded. Since the experiment was successful, it was repeated the following day and an official protocol was prepared. In the wake of the experiment, enough polyethylene had been produced by January 1936 to allow the properties of the product to be studied. This resulted in the discovery of the dielectric and film-forming properties of the material from which a thin yet robust product could be made. As a result, polyethylene emerged as a material that offered the potential for industrial use.

Broader interest in producing polyethylene arose only at this point. No later than August 1936, ICI filed an application for a patent to produce polyethylene, which the patent office granted in 1937, listing as inventors the team members from 1933 as well as the researcher who replicated the experiment in 1935. The patent also included suggested fields of application. Once the patent had been awarded, ICI embarked on an internal search between 1936 and 1938 for a specific use of the product. At the time, the usage deemed most likely to be successful was for the production of cable insulation, and in September 1938, the final decision was reached to commence large-scale production of polyethylene. Beginning in 1939, the most important customers were producers of electronic equipment for submarines. It was only after the Second World War, when the use of plastic bags began to spread, that polyethylene became a worldwide phenomenon. Indeed, it has been so successful that polyethylene pollution is one of the greatest environmental problems the world faces today (based on the discussion of the case in Radtke 2015).

Psychologist Karl Weick refers to this process of seeking goals after the fact as "sensemaking," in other words, the process of "making heads or tails out of something." In that respect, according to Weick (1987, 221), who references the work of Edward de Bono (1984, 143), strategy is best understood as luck that is rationalized after the fact. In Weick's view, the sense of an action or decision is frequently constructed retrospectively because one generally doesn't discover what purpose an activity actually serves until it has been performed. The classic, fundamental idea—and this infuriates instrumental-rationalists—could be formulated as, "How can I know what an organization's goals are, until I see the decisions being made inside of it?" Weick concludes that the task of management lies not so much in defining appropriate goals and deducing the means to achieve them, but rather in creating a framework within which the many diverse decisions made in the organization can be interpreted and ordered (Weick 1995, 9ff.).

The question that now presents itself is, what does a process of strategy formulation and strategy implementation look like if it takes such effects into consideration?

3.
Strategy Development beyond Understanding Organizations in Mechanistic Terms

Even the classical concepts of instrumental-rational strategy management admit that strategy processes often transpire in ways that are entirely different from their textbook descriptions. The criticism has been voiced that organizations sometimes do not pursue clear strategies, implement opposing strategies at the same time, change strategies very frequently, or employ strategies only for presentation to the outside world without putting them into effect internally. According to the classical understanding of strategy, however, all of this is seen as organizational pathology that can be managed through better planning or improved organizational design.

This approach, in fact, is one of the reasons for the growth programs of the major strategy consulting firms. Particularly at top management levels, where the (often dramatized) pressure of "turbulent markets," a "high degree of uncertainty," and the "hypercomplexity of the environment" is felt, the systematic processes that consultants offer as a means of searching for new and better resources promise at least a modicum of security. When one of the strategies developed with the consultants does not "take flight", this failure is not attributed to the instrumental-rational view of the organization. Instead, the next search process is launched with the assistance of other, or sometimes even the same, consultants.

Yet the problem is that the classical instrumental-rational approach is ill-suited for the development of strategies if the process is occurring under conditions of uncertainty. Often, glitches occur that could not have been imagined beforehand and frequently become even more aggravated through their consequences. This can result in fundamental changes for everyone involved, which is why prognoses of developments in the organization's fields of activity are unreliable (see Levy 1994, 170ff.). In brief, knowledge about the starting position is uncertain because there is insufficient information available, and the goal of the strategy process can only be formulated in vague terms.

For this reason, recent decades have seen suggestions for a fundamentally different approach to strategy processes that contrast with the instrumental-rational ideas still propagated by the major strategy consulting firms. Methods bearing names such as "logical incrementalism," the "learning strategy development," the "grassroots model of strategy development," "discursive strategy design," or "effectuation" are different in their details but are essentially based on a very similar approach.

3.1 The Emergence of the Approach

Our approach begins by unwinding the narrow instrumental-rational notion that suitable means are to be sought for a precisely defined goal. Organizational research has discovered that we draw false conclusions if we believe that the players who act rationally during strategy processes are actually seeking solutions for previously defined problems. In the majority of cases, they only have vague knowledge about the problems, the organization's goals are unclear or contradictory, and the decision-makers have come together somewhat accidentally. The problems, solutions, and players in a strategy process are only loosely connected with one another and have converged more or less by coincidence. Strategic decision-making processes are like a trash container that is full of problems, solutions, and players, binding with one another in a fairly arbitrary way (Cohen et al. 1972).

Granted, it is possible that, in the process, the solution to a specific problem is sought. Just as frequently, however—or even more frequently—we find people looking for a problem to fit a solution that already exists (see Starbuck 1982, 16f.). This is the case, for example, when a large number of important problems accumulate in an organization. In order to resolve the complexity arising from myriad problems, a player will seek a problem that is suitable for a solution that happens to be present at that moment anyway. Another situation arises when problems have needed a solution for some time, yet it has not been possible to assign an appropriate solution. Decision-makers simply shelve them until such time as a better opportunity to make a decision may present itself (Cohen et al. 1972). There are numerous examples of such forms of strategic decision-making.

To illustrate, when you look at the official accounts of scientific or business research processes, they often read as if the solution to a problem were being sought with the help of selected experts. In the meantime, scholarly research has shown that these processes often unfold in entirely different ways. Quite by chance, researchers may stumble upon a solution for which they don't even have a problem. They then consider formulating a question for which their solution might fit. The external presentation then conveys the impression –which is every bit in accordance with the instrumental-rational model—that the search involved the solution for a problem (or the means for an end). In reality, however, the scientific solution came first, and the scientific problem was only identified afterwards.

To draw on an historical example, if you take a superficial look at the genocide committed against European Jews, you might have the impression that the Nazis—very much in keeping with an instrumental-rational perspective—had a strategic master plan to annihilate this population and that constructing gas chambers in death camps in Treblinka, Bełżec, Sobibor, and Auschwitz appeared to be a suitable means to that end. In reality, the means to the end, killing with gas, came first. The Nazi regime had already been using this gas to euthanize the mentally ill and disabled as part of what was called the Aktion T4 program. After the conclusion of the Aktion T4 program, this complex of resources and personnel presented itself as a solution for other "problems." Alternative solutions to "the Jewish problem" (to quote the Nazi leadership's misanthropic formulation) turned out to be infeasible, for example, forced emigration to Madagascar, the establishment of reservations in the occupied Polish territories, or marching Jews into the Pripyat swamps or the tundra bordering the Polar Sea (Kühl 2014, 98).

EXAMPLE

Consulting Firms:
Finding Problems for Solutions That Already Exist

In a study on consulting projects in strategic personnel management, Alexander Gruber (2015) presents an example of post hoc assignment of managerial problems to means and solutions that already exist. In his case study, a team of business consultants always uses the same consulting approaches and management tools to address a range of strategic personnel problems in different consulting projects and firms. The consultants have a "pool of material" which contains appropriate presentation and working materials for a wide variety of inquiries and assignments including a sizable inventory of presentation slides, questionnaires, diagrams, and personnel management tools such as personal portfolios, competency catalogs, and personnel flowcharts.

Although these tools were originally developed from pre-existing modular components for individual, distinct project situations and in the context of specific problems, they gradually condensed into generalized consulting tools. As such, they developed a certain value in themselves that was exploited in different project settings and even during acquisition attempts.

In the various projects, the tool set is then adjusted to the client's relevant needs, but only partially, for example, by taking an org chart from a previous assignment and inserting the matching number of employees. And yet, the conceptual

> structure of the management tools, along with the competence profiles, personnel portfolios, and personnel flow charts, always remains the same. In this manner, tools that were developed for specific situations gradually morph into a generally tried-and-tested, strategically effective set of tools that accompanies the consulting team from one project to the next.

Approaches such as "logical incrementalism," "learning strategy development," the "grassroots model of strategy development," "discursive strategy development," or "effectuation" do not attempt to use an instrumental-rational form of strategy design to replace decision processes which can repeatedly be found in reality. Instead, they try to exert influence on these "wild" decision processes within the framework of a strategy process.

What does that mean in concrete terms?

3.2 Searching for the Means to an End as well as Searching for an End for Existing Means

In the approach we favor, the objective is to set up the strategy development process in a way that identifies resources necessary to achieve previously defined goals, yet also in a way that the organization remains open to searching for appropriate goals for existing means. The task, in other words, is not to forgo the classical method of formulating strategies—as a search for the means to accomplish defined goals—but also to reflect on the search for goals with existing means. This is unusual for many organizations.

The first method, namely, searching for the means to realize previously defined goals, is what organizations frequently choose intuitively when they hear the word strategy. It entails defining a goal upon which as many people as possible can agree. Then there are deliberations, with or without the help of consultants, as to which means—or strategies, to use a different term—can be used to achieve the goal. Under many circumstances, this method can make sense for an organization. Often there are precisely defined goals for which suitable means must be found. Let's say an organization is assigned the task of attracting the Olympic Games to a certain location. That is an unequivocal goal and it makes no sense to act as if the objective were not to find suitable resources to reach it.

In the strategy discussion, this is called the "greenhouse model" of strategy formulation (Mintzberg/McHugh 1985). Before a greenhouse is planned and built, the planners decide on which kinds of vegetables they would like to grow; they then search for the best means to reach their goal, which is to grow those kinds of vegetables most economically. The greenhouse is then constructed according to the plans, and in the end a review is undertaken to verify that the designated number of tomatoes, cucumbers, or paprika can be harvested each day.

The second approach, the creation of goals for existing means, fundamentally reverses this logic. Here, the question revolves around which means are currently available in the organization and could be used as a basis to pursue various goals. We do not ask whether the resources are present to fulfill a goal; instead, we ask whether we have the resources to drive a promising development ahead. This does not include calculation of the expected earnings (which assumes a precise goal), but rather of the losses that could be incurred in a worst-case scenario (see Sarasvathy 2001, 245ff.). This method is useful when goals cannot be readily set because the organization itself is not yet clear on how the field might develop, or because the goals must still be negotiated and agreed upon with other players (see March 1976, 74ff.). When a company that has been financed with venture capital tries out a new product in a new kind of market, it has no way of knowing how things will turn out in the end. The company's job is to press ahead with a range of developments and see which one gains traction.

This approach is also called the grassroots model of strategy formulation (Mintzberg/McHugh 1985). It is said that strategies proliferate like weeds in a garden; they take root in unusual places in and even outside of the garden. Sometimes a weed is so successful that it takes over the entire garden. Sometimes the gardener then removes the weeds, although there are cases where they are allowed to spread and perhaps are even encouraged to do so. In most cases, however, the weeds die of their own accord because they cannot survive in their locations.

In most strategy processes it makes little sense to choose only one path or the other. Rather, the objective is to link the two methods.

3.3 Strategic Testing—Resolving the Divide between Strategy Development and Strategy Implementation

"Logical incrementalism," "learning strategy development," "discursive strategy design," and "effectuation" share the basic idea of beginning with small measures before evaluating various alternatives. In this respect, these approaches differ fundamentally from the classical method of strategy development, which advocates that we should assess the various alternative means first and only begin with implementation afterwards (for a critical perspective on the classical method, see Bourgeois/Brodwin 1984; Hart/Banbury 1994).

There are a range of names for this tentative, step-by-step manner in a strategy development process. Some refer to it as "patching," in other words, stitching together an organizational strategy. The concept of "sprints" has trickled into the strategy debate from the field of software development. This involves developing a completely functional measure over a very short period of time in order to determine whether or not it will prove itself in practice. We also use the term "incrementing" in connection with strategy processes to indicate that individual steps can be addressed independently of one another. The most accessible concept, however, is presumably that of "testing" because it convincingly suggests that one deliberately leaves the question open as to whether a measure will succeed.

This method does not entail the preparation of a master plan for achieving the desired goal. Instead, once the possible approaches have been reviewed, you simply start a series of trials. The advantage of this method lies in its ability to test smaller measures that can either be phased out or cancelled without incurring major losses. One of the first people to bring the method into play was Charles Lindblom (1965, 143ff.). His idea was that testing should always address individual problems only, and that the solution of the individual problems would then serve as a basis for the development of a more or less consistent overall strategy.

The advantage of this method is that at the beginning of the testing a broad consensus is not required within the organization about the goals to be accomplished or their means. In the framework of a strategy process, this spares the organization from having to make a binding decision for every measure, a procedure that is often very difficult in situations that are micro-politically charged.

In contrast to the classical strategy process, there are no objective criteria for the "right strategy" here. If agreement has been reached about the testing—even if it is only in the form of tolerating it, or a standstill agreement—then the testing is initially taken into consideration as a "feasible path" (see Schreyögg 1984, 222). Hence, whether a test is suitable for the organization is not something that is determined beforehand, but it becomes evident when the measure either does or does not gain traction.

There is a fable involving bees and flies that is used to illustrate why testing makes managerial sense in a strategy process. The story goes like this: if you put a half-dozen bees and a half-dozen flies in an open bottle and position it so that the bottom of the bottle is facing the sun, the bees will try to find an opening in the closed bottom until they die of exhaustion. Meanwhile, within a few minutes the flies will figure out that they can escape through the neck of the bottle. The relatively intelligent bees had a problem: they were trying to find an escape route systematically, relying on the strategy that appears most logical them. The flies, which are significantly less intelligent and don't even try to develop a goal-oriented strategy, arrive at a workable solution automatically, as it were, by wildly flying back and forth (among other places, the story can be found in Peters/Waterman 1982, 108, or Mintzberg et al. 1999, 207).

3.4 The Process Architecture for the Development of Strategies: The Resolution of the Classical Phase Model

The approach suggested here amounts to a departure from the classical strategy process and its linear course of action. Instead of going through the sequential phases of goal setting, exploration, current state analysis, hypothesis formation, detailed concept elaboration, decision-making, implementation, and success monitoring, the process steps are interwoven. At the beginning, only a rough goal is set in the form of a goal corridor, which is split in two. The current state analysis, hypothesis formation, detailed concept elaboration, decision-making, testing, implementation, and success monitoring phases run, for the most part, parallel to one another.

For these reasons, strategy implementation is integrated into strategy development. The result is that we avoid the breaks between development and implementation that are common in classical strategy development processes. In comparison to classical linear strategy processes, concept development, testing, and feedback processes run simultaneously, permitting the strategy process to be accelerated.

This process architecture also shifts the importance of the players involved in the strategy process. Seen from this perspective, the driving forces behind an organization's reorientation are the operative units (see Noda/Bower 1996, 161). It tends to be the lower and mid-level managers who are in a position to identify, implement and evaluate opportunities for small-scale testing.

The role of top-level management is to act more as a "catalyst for the development of new strategies." No longer required to be fully in charge of the strategic process, senior management "recognizes the widespread process of idea generation and decision making" and attempts, for one thing, to influence it proactively by setting the "rules of the game" (see Schreyögg 1998, 41f.). The objective is therefore no longer to plan and supervise the processes of strategy development and formulation from above. Instead, within the framework of "meta-management" or "meta-planning," top management outlines the scope of the strategy development, addresses the various "suggestions," "impulses," or "strategy formulations," and then reviews, selects, and ensures that even competing initiatives can be moved ahead (Schreyögg 1998, 42).

According to this perspective, the organization's strategy planners and consultants cannot claim that they are "better" at formulating a strategy than the decentralized units of the organization. Granted, by engaging the units of the organization they can attempt to gain access to information, suggest formulations for strategies, and then try to push them through by enlisting the hierarchical power at the top of the organization. Ultimately, however, most of the strategies that are formulated "up above" will peter out during the implementation phase or, worse yet, fail the test of practical reality. The planning staff and consultants therefore play a role akin to that of a midwife who assists the decentralized units to give birth to their ideas (Schnelle 2006). Ideas often remain vague in the minds of their initiators, and the task of the planning staff and consultants is to elaborate them in such a way that they can and must be dealt with.

4.
Concerning the Classification of Strategy Processes: Goals as a Characteristic of Structure, among Other Things

Adherents of the instrumental-rational perspective on strategy processes need not be irritated by such diverse critiques of their view of organizations, with its orientation toward goal optimization. If an organization decides to try out end-means reversals, they can use a strategy retreat to call for reflection on the organization's original goals. In the event that focusing on two contradictory goals prevents a streamlined rationalization of processes, then they can demand a clear strategy of splitting into two different organizations, each of which has its own distinct purpose.

This enables an organization to use its own day-to-day operations to immunize itself against the various insecurities entailed by the classical instrumental model. The motto could be: if reality does not correspond to my PowerPoint slides with their straightforward end-means model, then too bad for practical reality. Managers, consultants, and researchers use this divergence as an occasion to call for "clearer goals," "precise goal definition," and "the resolution of goal conflicts." In strategy processes, the goal becomes a kind of fetish that is adhered to in the organizational analysis. Watching the situation unfold, we are reminded of Sisyphus, who repeatedly tries to roll the stone of ever new strategy processes up the hill of instrumental-rationality, even though the stone always, always slips out of control. Yet a heretic might note that it is precisely this eternal failure due to one's own demands for rationality that keeps Sisyphus in motion and keeps the strategists among managers and consultants busy. And to a certain degree that is probably also a good thing; just remember the concept of organizational blinders.

Classical strategy theory paints a picture of the instrumental-rational organization that is no more than a simplified caricature of organizational reality. Admittedly, the picture of organizations as consisting of end-means relationships is simple, neatly arranged, and understandable. It is relatively easy to analyze organizations on the basis of this image. Depending on the complexity of the problem, we need only a greater or lesser amount of computing capacity and a larger or smaller number of strategy experts, or research assistants, to "calculate" the proper strategic solution for an organization. The advantages notwithstanding, this picture of organizations has little to do with reality.

It is more productive to inquire into the logic behind all of these "contaminations" of the classical, goal-focused picture of organizations. Why do shifts in goals, the continuing existence of an organization regardless of success or failure in goal achievement, and end-means reversals makes sense? What is the rationale behind focusing on several competing goals? Why are organizations unable to do without formulations that are as attractive as possible but contribute little to guiding decision-making?

Imagine that the dream of instrumental rationalists, namely, organizational alignment with a single goal, actually came true.

The problem can be illustrated using human beings. Presumably, the exclusive and rigid pursuit of a single goal would make a person go to pieces. A researcher who saw the sole meaning of her life as the solution of one of the world's scientific mysteries would at some point have to be fed artificially because an occupation as banal as taking nutrition would seem unimportant to her. In a sense, she would be externally forced to take other goals seriously.

In spite of this—and this point is important for the discussion of strategy—people cannot treat goals in a completely erratic fashion either. Goal rigidity can ruin a person, but you can also founder because you lack the ability to concentrate on one goal, and one goal only, for at least a short period of time. An employee who finds herself in a meeting devoted to positioning a new electric toothbrush will encounter acceptance problems if her attention continuously, not just occasionally, wanders to other interesting thoughts, such as the romantic experiences of the night before, beating a video game record, or the dishwasher that still remains unloaded. Conversely, an executive who is having a romantic dinner with his new love interest will encounter acceptance problems if telephone calls, text messages, and emails continually remind him of his other responsibilities, and he is no longer certain which goal he should actually pursue.

In practical terms, *opportunistic goal setting* is predominant, the more or less abrupt adjustment of goals to suit existing opportunities and constraints (see Cyert/March 1963, 35f. and 118). Depending on which pressures or opportunities present themselves, we switch back and forth between different goals. If people happen to be in love, then they let work slide a little. By the same token, it's well known that the best books are written during phases when one is not distracted by the day-to-day chaos of a romance. Sometimes it's business before pleasure, and sometimes just the reverse.

Goals represent one of the possible ways to program an organization, but only *one* of them. Goals can also function as guiding parameters, for example, in the search for suitable personnel or for assigning them meaningful positions. Yet it can also happen that one already has the employee and is looking for suitable tasks, a goal, for her—or that the number of available positions is considered a "symbol for the size and importance of an organizational unit" and tasks and personnel are being sought for them (see Luhmann 2000, 235).

From this vantage point, the many deviations from a single-purpose orientation no longer appear to be pathological, as they do in the classic instrumental-rational model, but rather as expressions of organizational adaptability. The conscious or unconscious goal switching, the continuing existence of organizations regardless of their success or failure in achieving their goals, the reversal of ends and means, as well as the use of goals to justify decisions after the fact, are all expressions of an organization's intelligence.

Bibliography

Allen, James Albert. 1967. *Studies in Innovation in the Steel and Chemical Industries*. Manchester: Manchester University Press.

Amburgey, Terry L., and Tina Dacin. 1994. "As the Left Foot Follows the Right? The Dynamics of Strategic and Structural Change." *Academy of Management Journal* 37:1427–52.

Bono, Edward de. 1984. *Tactics: The Art and Science of Success*. Boston: Little, Brown & Company.

Bourgeois, L. J., and David R. Brodwin. 1984. "Strategic Implementation: Five Approaches to an Elusive Phenomenon." *Strategic Management Journal* 5:241–64.

Burgelman, Robert A. 1994. "Fading Memories: A Process Theory of Strategic Business Exit in Dynamic Environments." *Administrative Science Quarterly* 39:24–56.

Burgelman, Robert A., and Andrew Grove. 1996. "Strategic Dissonance." *California Management Review* 38:8–25.

Chandler, Alfred D. 1962. *Strategy and Structure*. Cambridge: MIT Press.

Cloutier, Charlotte, and Richard Whittington. 2013. "Strategy-as-Practice." In *Encyclopedia of Management Theory*, edited by Eric H. Kessler, 803–6. Los Angeles/London/New Delhi/Singapore/Washington, D.C.: Sage.

Cohen, Michael D., James G. March, and Johan P. Olsen. 1972. "A Garbage Can Model of Rational Choice." *Administrative Science Quarterly* 17:1–25.

Cyert, Richard M., and James G. March. 1963. *A Behavioral Theory of the Firm*. Englewood Cliffs: Prentice-Hall.

Cyert, Richard M., and James G. March. 1992. *A Behavioral Theory of the Firm*. Cambridge: Blackwell.

David, Robert J. 2012. "Institutional Change and the Growth of Strategy Consulting in the United States." In *Management Consulting*, edited by Matthias Kipping and Timothy Clark, 71–92. Oxford/New York: Oxford University Press.

Doran, George T. 1981. "There's a S.M.A.R.T. Way to Write Management's Goals and Objectives." *Management Review* 70:35–36.

Drucker, Peter F. 1964. *Managing for Results*. New York: Harper & Row.

Georgiu, Petro. 1973. "The Goal Paradigm and Notes toward a Counter Paradigm." *Administrative Science Quarterly* 18:291–310.

Goold, Michael, and Andrew Campbell. 1987. *Strategies and Styles: The Role of the Centre in Managing Diversified Corporations*. Oxford: Blackwell.

Gross, Edward. 1969. "The Definition of Organizational Goals." *British Journal of Sociology* 20:277–94.

Gruber, Alexander. 2015. *Beraten nach Zahlen:* Über Steuerungsinstrumente und Kennzahlen in Beratungsprojekten. Wiesbaden: VS Verlag für Sozialwissenschaften.

Hall, David, and Maurice A. Saias. 1980. "Strategy Follows Structure!" *Strategic Management Journal* 1:149–63.

Hamel, Gary. 1998. "Strategy Innovation and the Quest for Value." *Sloan Management Review* 39:7–14.

Hart, Stuart, and Catherine Banbury. 1994. "How Strategy-Making Processes Can Make a Difference." *Strategic Management Journal* 15:251–69.

Hendry, John, and David Seidl. 2003. "The Structure and Significance of Strategic Episodes: Social Systems Theory and the Routine Practices of Strategic Change." *Journal of Management Studies* 40:175–96.

Hofer, Charles W., and Dan Schendel. 1978. *Strategy Formulation: Analytical Concepts.* St. Paul: West Publishing Company.

Hunger, J. David, and Thomas L. Wheelen. 1996. *Strategic Management.* Reading/Menlo Park/New York: Addison-Wesley.

Hussey, David. 1998. *Strategic Management: From Theory to Implementation.* Oxford/Boston/Johannesburg: Butterworth Heinemann.

Inkpen, Andrew, and Nandan Choudhury. 1995. "The Seeking of Strategy Where It Is Not: Towards a Theory of Strategy Absence." *Strategic Management Journal* 16:313–23.

Jarzabkowski, Paula, Julia Balogun, and David Seidl. 2007. "Strategizing: The Challenge of a Practice Perspective." *Human Relations* 60:5–27.

Kaplan, Robert, and David P. Norton. 2001. *The Strategy-Focused Organization: How Balanced Scorecard Companies Thrive in the New Business Environment.* Boston: Harvard Business School Press.

Kieser, Alfred, and Lars Leiner. 2009. *On the Impossibility of Collaborative Research—and on the Usefulness of Researchers and Practitioners Irritating Each Other.* Mannheim: unpublished manuscript.

Kirsch, Werner. 1997. *Strategisches Management.* Herrsching: Barbara Kirsch Verlag.

Kolbusa, Matthias. 2012. *Der Strategie-Scout: Komplexität beherrschen, Szenarien nutzen, Politik machen.* Wiesbaden: Gabler.

Kühl, Stefan. 2013. *Organizations: A Systems Approach*. Farnham: Gower.

Kühl, Stefan. 2014. *Ganz normale Organisationen: Zur Soziologie des Holocaust*. Berlin: Suhrkamp.

Levy, David. 1994. "Chaos Theory and Strategy: Theory, Application, and Managerial Implications." *Strategic Management Journal* 15:167–78.

Lindblom, Charles E. 1965. *The Intelligence of Democracy*. New York: Macmillan.

Luhmann, Niklas. 1964a. *Funktionen und Folgen formaler Organisation*. Berlin: Duncker & Humblot.

Luhmann, Niklas. 1964b. "Zweck – Herrschaft – System: Grundbegriffe und Prämissen Max Webers." *Der Staat* 3:129–58.

Luhmann, Niklas. 1971. "Reform des öffentlichen Dienstes." In *Politische Planung*, edited by Niklas Luhmann, 203–56. Opladen: WDV.

Luhmann, Niklas. 1972. *Rechtssoziologie*. Reinbek: Rowohlt.

Luhmann, Niklas. 1973. *Zweckbegriff und Systemrationalität*. Frankfurt a.M.: Suhrkamp.

Luhmann, Niklas. 1981. "Organisation im Wirtschaftssystem." In *Soziologische Aufklärung 3: Soziales System, Gesellschaft, Organisation*, edited by Niklas Luhmann, 390–414. Opladen: WDV.

Luhmann, Niklas. 1984. *Soziale Systeme*. Frankfurt a.M.: Suhrkamp.

Luhmann, Niklas. 1988. "Organisation." In *Mikropolitik: Macht und Spiele in Organisationen*, edited by Willi Küpper and Günther Ortmann, 165–186, Opladen: WDV.

Luhmann, Niklas. 2000. *Organisation und Entscheidung*. Opladen: WDV.

Luhmann, Niklas. 2016. *Der neue Chef*. Berlin: Suhrkamp.

March, James G. 1976. "The Technology of Foolishness." In *Ambiguity and Choice in Organizations*, edited by James G. March and Johan P. Olsen, 69–81. Bergen: Universitetsforlaget.

March, James G. 2015. "The First 50 Years and the Next 50 Years of A Behavioral Theory of the Firm: An Interview with James G. March." *Journal of Management Inquiry* 24:149–55.

Mintzberg, Henry. 1978. "Patterns in Strategy Formation." *Management Science* 24:934–48.

Mintzberg, Henry. 1987. "Crafting Strategy." *Harvard Business Review* 4:66–75.

Mintzberg, Henry. 1990. "Strategy Formation: Schools of Thought." In *Perspectives on Strategic Management*, edited by J.W. Fredrickson, 105–235. New York: Harper & Row.

Mintzberg, Henry. 1990. "The Design School: Reconsidering the Basic Promises of Strategic Management." *Strategic Management Journal* 11:171–95.

Mintzberg, Henry. 1994. *The Rise and Fall of Strategic Planning*. New York: Free Press.

Mintzberg, Henry. 2014. "Five Ps for Strategy." In *The Strategy Process: Concepts, Contexts, Cases*, edited by Joseph Lampel, Henry Mintzberg, James B. Quinn, and Sumantra Ghoshal, 3–9. Harlow/London/New York: Pearson.

Mintzberg, Henry, and Alexandra McHugh. 1985. "Strategy Formation in an Adhocracy." *Administrative Science Quarterly* 30: 180–97.

Mintzberg, Henry, and James A. Waters. 1985. "Of Strategies, Deliberate and Emergent." *Strategic Management Journal* 6: 257–72.

Mintzberg, Henry, Bruce Ahlstrand, Bruce, and Joseph Lampel. 2005. *Strategy Safari: A Guided Tour Through The Wilds of Strategic Management.* New York/London/Toronto/Sidney: Simon and Schuster.

Noda, Tomo, and Jospeh L. Bower. 1996. "Strategy Making as Iterated Processes of Resource Allocation." *Strategic Management Journal* 17:159–92.

Nordsieck, Fritz. 1932. *Die schaubildliche Erfassung und Untersuchung der Betriebsorganisation.* Stuttgart: C.E. Poeschel.

Perrow, Charles. 1961. "The Analysis of Goals in Complex Organizations." *American Sociological Review* 26:854–66.

Peters, Thomas J., and Robert H. Waterman. 1982. *In Search of Excellence.* New York: Harper & Row.

Pfeffer, Jeffrey, and Gerald R. Salancik. 1978. *The External Control of Organizations: A Resource Dependence Perspective.* New York: Harper & Row.

Prahalad, C. K., and Gary Hamel. 1990. "The Core Competence of the Corporation." *Harvard Business Review* 68:79–91.

Quinn, James B. 2014. "Strategies for Change." In *The Strategy Process: Concepts, Contexts, Cases*, edited by Joseph Lampel, Henry Mintzberg, James B. Quinn, and Sumantra Ghoshal, 9–15. Harlow/London/New York: Pearson.

Radtke, Jacqueline. 2015. *Strategie jenseits zweckrationaler Verengungen: Fallbeispiele.* Bielefeld: unpublished manuscript.

Rumelt, Richard. 2011. *Good Strategy, Bad Strategy: The Difference and Why it Matters.* New York: Crown Business.

Sarasvathy, Saras D. 2001. "Causation and Effectuation: Toward a Theoretical Shift from Economic Inevitability to Entrepreneurial Contingency." *Academy of Management Review* 26:243–63.

Schendel, Dan E., and Charles W. Hofer. 1979. *Strategic Management: A New View of Business Policy and Planning*. Boston: Little, Brown & Company.

Schilling, Melissa A. 2013. *Strategic Management of Technological Innovation*. New York: McGraw-Hill Irwin.

Schnelle, Wolfgang. 2006. *Diskursive Organisations- und Strategieberatung*. Norderstedt: BoD.

Schreyögg, Georg. 1984. *Unternehmensstrategie: Grundfragen einer Theorie strategischer Unternehmensführung*. Berlin/New York: Walter de Gruyter.

Schreyögg, Georg. 1998. "Strategische Diskurse: Strategieentwicklung im organisatorischen Prozess." *Organisationsentwicklung* 17:32–43.

Seidl, David. 2007. "General Strategy Concepts and the Ecology of Strategy Discourses: A Systemic-Discursive Perspective." *Organization Studies* 28:197–218.

Simon, Herbert A. 1957. *Administrative Behavior*. New York: The Free Press.

Starbuck, William H. 1982. "Congealing Oil: Inventing Ideologies to Justify Acting Ideologies Out." *Journal of Management Studies* 19:3–27.

Stewart, Matthew. 2009. *The Management Myth: Why the Experts Keep Getting it Wrong*. New York: Norton.

Thompson, James D., and William J. McEwen. 1958. "Organizational Goals and Environment." *American Sociological Review* 23:23–31.

Weber, Max. 1976. *Wirtschaft und Gesellschaft*. Tübingen: J.C.B. Mohr.

Weick, Karl E. 1987. "Substitutes for Corporate Strategy." In *The Competitive Challenge: Strategies for Industrial Innovation and Renewal*, edited by David J. Teece, 221–33. Cambridge: Ballinger.

Weick, Karl E. 1995. *Sensemaking in Organizations*. Thousand Oaks/London/New Delhi: Sage.

Whitley, Richard. 1984. "The Scientific Status of Management Research as a Practically-Oriented Social Science." *Journal of Management Studies* 21:369–90.

Whittington, Richard. 1993. *What Is Strategy and Does It Matter*. London/New York: Routledge.

Whittington, Richard. 1996. "Strategy as Practice." *Long Range Planning* 29:731–35.

Whittington, Richard. 2003. "The Work of Strategizing and Organizing: For a Practice Perspective." *Strategic Organization* 1:117–25.

Whittington, Richard. 2006. "Completing the Practice Turn in Strategy Research." *Organization Studies* 27:613–34.

www.ingramcontent.com/pod-product-compliance
Lightning Source LLC
Chambersburg PA
CBHW020302030426
42336CB00010B/868